THE WORLD'S RAILROADS
HIGH-SPEED TRAINS

THE WORLD'S RAILROADS
HIGH-SPEED TRAINS

By Christopher Chant; edited by John Moore

Chelsea House Publishers
Philadelphia

Published in 2000 by
Chelsea House Publishers
1974 Sproul Road, Suite 400
P.O. Box 914
Broomall. PA 19008-0914

ISBN 0-7910-5565-5

Printed in China

TITLE PAGES: British Rail diesel-electric HST (High Speed Train).

OPPOSITE: SNCF (Société Nationale des Chemins de Fer Français) electric-powered train.

HIGH-SPEED TRAINS

As the year 2000 approached, one of the most far-sighted railroad concepts to be entertained for many years, initiated in 1996, was coming to fruition in Europe as a collaborative venture by Belgium, France, Germany, the Netherlands and the United Kingdom. Based in Belgium, the 10-year plan was conceived to create high-speed rail links connecting Paris, Brussels, Köln (Cologne), Amsterdam and London. This PBKAL project is making good progress, and it was anticipated that all the proposed links would by fully operational by 2005, although some parts, such as the links between Brussels and Antwerp and between Brussels and Liège, should be established by 2002, and the tunnel connecting the northern and southern railroad stations in Antwerp should be ready for traffic by 2003.

However, though many of the most fascinating railway developments are those taking shape in the western part of Europe, the development of the 'railroad culture' is not restricted to the more affluent countries of the northern hemisphere. In the developing countries of the southern hemisphere there have developed a number of railroads reflecting the desire of such countries to exploit their natural resources,

OPPOSITE: A Rail Europe TVG (Train Grande Vitesse) Duplex.

RIGHT: The Eurostar high-speed trains run between London and Paris and Brussels through the Channel Tunnel.

and typical of these nations is Brazil, where new railroad lines have been developed into the rain forests of the Amazon basin. The creation of this type of infrastructure should be (but in some cases has not been) balanced by efforts to counter the adverse environmental consequences of such developments. Railroad development in Africa has been spasmodic and singularly poorly planned in overall terms, and although the continent's nations that have gained independence in the last 35 years have indeed invested in railroads, in overall terms the development of the continent's railroad network has been hampered by the devil's brew of general political instability, frequent civil war and constant lack of resources.

The development of the railroad system in China has been greater than that of anywhere else in the world: since 1949 and the end of the civil war that saw the defeat of the ruling nationalist party by the communists, the country's network has been extended by more than 30,000 miles (48280km). This development is not to the main-line network, for other elements of modern railroad thinking have entered the Chinese transport equation in the form of a growing number of 'light rail' and

underground railroad projects. Typical of the latter, for instance, is the plan for the system in the southern city of Shenzhen, a 9.5-mile (15-km) network extending under the city proper to the outlying suburb of Futian, linking Lowu and Lok Ma Chau. This advanced system will make it possible for passengers to travel from Hong Kong into the centre of the city in only some 20 minutes. In Hong Kong itself, construction began late in 1998 on the first element of the region's new West Rail Project and, on completion, this double-track electrified system will cover some 21 miles (34km) from Yen Chow Street in Kowloon to Tuen Mun: a notable aspect of the system, designed to provide no interference with the already overcrowded road system of this ex-British colony, is the fact that while 8.5 miles (13.7km) will be underground some 5.5 miles (8.8km) of the rest of the network will be elevated. It is planned that the system will possess nine stations, including two providing the possibility of interchange with the main-line railroad between Kowloon and Beijing. Hong Kong is also the recipient of a new 21.1-mile (34-km) 'light rail' system, in this instance connecting the new Chek Lap Kok airport on Lantau island with Kowloon and

providing, as a world 'first', check-in facilities at its various stations.

As the world's railroad systems continue to grow in importance from the decline evident in the middle 50 years of the 20th century, the revival of rail transport is now seen in a somewhat different light, especially among the nations of the Western world. The desirability of railroad transport is not regarded exclusively as a factor of economic importance, but also as an element of the social and ecological significance increasingly attached to the curtailment of the importance that has until very recently been attached to the motor vehicle as the pre-eminent means of moving people and goods both within and between urban centres. There is now far greater emphasis on the creation of integrated road and rail transport systems that will lessen pollution by reducing the numbers of private cars and trucks gridlocking urban streets, and ease national levels of congestion and social irritability by trimming the numbers of private cars and trucks using the road network. In short, the concept that has developed is that neither the motor vehicle nor the train should exercise a dominant influence on transport policy as they once did in successive periods, but that the railroad should become a major partner to the motor vehicle within the context of an integrated approach to the creation of a transport system that serves the needs of the population.

Rising traffic congestion and its attendant pollution have placed emphasis on the establishment of a viable alternative to

ABOVE: Hong Kong has one of the best suburban railroad systems in the world, this being part of the line connecting Kowloon with Hong Kong proper.

OPPOSITE: As this photograph nicely reveals, the Chinese railroad system is comprehensively integrated into the everyday lives of the Chinese workers who have to use it.

the vital qualities of life for urban populations, much work has still to be done in improving matters and, perhaps just as importantly, persuading potential railroad travellers that the train has much to offer as an alternative to the car.

Though the perception of the significance of railroad use as a social and ecological tool to reduce the reliance of the Western world on the motor vehicle is most generally seen in terms of relevance to ownership and use of the private motor car, it is in fact of equal importance in terms of reducing the extent to which trucks and other heavy road vehicles are needed. In its capacity as the means of moving large loads, the railroad has seen something of a renaissance, albeit a limited one, with a number of important changes evident in its operations. From the 1960s the method of sending freight by railroad in individual wagons, the standard concept since the dawn of the railroad age, has become considerably less popular as obsolescent ways of handling freight, in which the railroads concentrated on the running of bulk movements of one particular type of load, whether a unitary mass such as coal or a fragmented mass such as a mixture of goods, allowed road competition to steal away business. The carrying of bulk loads is among the most cogent arguments for railroad development, for every railroad load trims the number of trucks on the world's roads. The delivery of bulk loads of coal, stone and other mass items such as mineral ores is still one of the railroad's most important economic offerings, and has

road transport by railroads that can operate services that provide the right blend of cleanliness, convenience, affordability and efficiency. It is only if they can provide this combination of attributes that the railroads stand any realistic chance of persuading motorists to switch to railroad transport. The growth and importance of 'light rail' and metro tram systems in the world's largest conurbations have indicated that although railways can make a difference to

become financially more attractive as railroad technology enhancements have made it possible to operate longer and heavier trains.

In the U.S.A. and other parts of the world such as Australia, China and the southern part of Africa, the movement of bulk loads by railroad is far more significant than it is in Europe. In the U.S.A., the Burlington Northern Railroad (now the Burlington Northern Santa Fe Railroad) introduced a train that delivered a load weighing more than 11,000 tons in 100 wagons. In South Africa, trains of up to some 20,000 tons are hauled some 550 miles (885km) from the Sishen iron-ore mines to the port of Saldanha: a fascinating aspect of these trains is that a motorcycle is carried on each of the five locomotives, allowing the crew to make regular inspections of the train, which can be more than 1.5 miles (2.4km) long.

In their attempts to boost the freight business, railroad operators have considered a number of unorthodox concepts. The idea of the TOFC ('Trailer On Flat Car') started in the U.S.A., permits truck trailer units to be carried on flatcars, and during the 1970s American and Canadian railroads were dealing with slightly less than 2 million TOFC loads each year. Problems with loading gauges precluded the use of such innovations in the U.K. and continental Europe until recent times, but in 1996 proposals were put forward for 'piggyback' trains of the North American pattern to become operational by 1999.

Another chance helping to transform

the nature and extent of freight transport by railroad has been the spread of containerization. The widespread use of containers for the movement of freight all over the world, and the adaptability of the container for movement by ship, railroad and truck has constituted a genuine revolution in the way freight is handled. In the U.S.A. extremely long trains of flatcars are used to deliver vast numbers of containers between the east and west coasts, and between the Great Lakes and the Gulf of Mexico, for it makes better economic

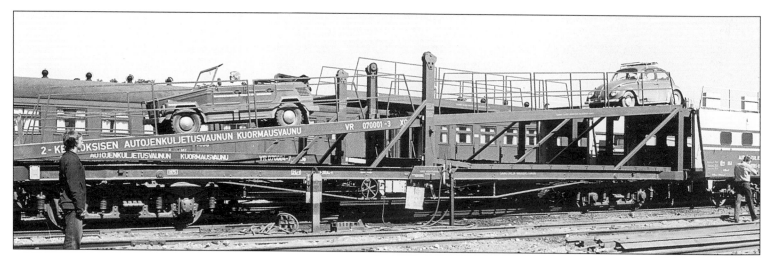

ABOVE: *Unloading passengers' cars from a Finnish State Railways car-carrying train.*

LEFT: *A truck being loaded onto a German Deutsche Bundesbahn 'piggyback' train.*

OPPOSITE
ABOVE LEFT: *A special car-carrying unit on a passenger train of the Finnish State Railways.*

ABOVE RIGHT: *DB piggyback wagons permit the long-distance, high-speed transport of goods while still aboard these truck trailers.*

BELOW RIGHT: *Imported cars being loaded onto a Santa Fe Autoveyor at Long Beach, California for shipment east.*

sense to do this than ship the containers via the Panama Canal or via the St. Lawrence Seaway. The monumental size of this effort can be ascertained from the fact that each of these trains is generally more than 1 mile (1.6km) long, and is hauled by no fewer than six locomotives. The extent and importance of container traffic in the U.K. has also grown enormously, and was originally given the brand name 'Freightliner' by British Railways in a very real perception of the business's essential nature, and today is just as important to the British railway business, especially since the opening of the Channel Tunnel and the consequent facilitation of rapid rail transport to and from the European mainland, where container freight has also become increasingly the norm for bulk delivery.

The concept of genuinely integrated transport links is also highly relevant to the modern freight transport business, and as a result there have appeared ever increasing numbers of regional 'intermodal' freight depots, and still more are planned: such intermodal depots greater improve the interchangeability of freight between the road and railroad networks, and are located strategically in regions where nodes of the two types of freight movement exist comfortably close to each other.

Despite the resurgence in the use of the railroad for the movement of freight, it is the railroad's capability in terms of high-speed passenger transport that has caught the eye of the public to a far greater extent. This is largely the result of the advanced, even futuristic, lines of the special trains developed for the task, the gaudy liveries in which such trains operate, and the very high speeds at which such trains run on services that are considerably faster than those of the private motor car. The high-speed railroad services are admittedly slower than those offered by the regional passenger aircraft that are their main rivals, but the railroad services have the advantage of

ABOVE LEFT: *Potash train east of Lytton, British Columbia.*

ABOVE: *A Canadian Pacific freight train on the Notch Hill Loop, British Columbia.*

LEFT: *Another Candian Pacific freight train crossing the Lethbridge viaduct over the Oldman river in Alberta.*

OPPOSITE

LEFT: *Configuration of tracks at the west end of Santa Fe's computerized classification yard at Barstow, east of Los Angeles, California, showing simultaneous arrivals and departures without interference.*

RIGHT: *A heavy freight train of the Canadian Pacific Railway wends its way through the Rocky Mountains, the beauty of the scenery unseen by all except the crews of the locomotives.*

operating at a high average speed from city centre to city centre, whereas the regional aircraft operators have to contend with the fact that their passengers must first travel out of the city centre to book into their service, then often have to wait before take-off, and then reverse the whole process at the other end of the service. The operators of high-speed railroad services can therefore offer point-to-point services between city centres cheaper but not notably slower than those of the airlines.

The best known of these high-speed services anywhere in the world are those provided by the Train Grande Vitesse (TGV), a French train which travels so fast that special lines had to be laid with greater than normal spacing between the tracks to reduce the buffeting which ensues when the trains pass each other. Another feature of the line is that they conform closely to the terrain contours and thus avoid the need in most cases for tunnels. The tracks are also built with a special camber that permits curves to be negotiated safely at very high speed. Movement on the TGV, between Paris and southern France and Switzerland, is so smooth that not only is the impression of the high speed hard to judge, but there is also little chance to study the local scenery. This journey takes a breathtaking 4 hours 32 minutes. Combining *Eurostar* and TGV services, the passenger can depart London at 9.53 a.m., reach Paris at 2.08 p.m. via the Channel Tunnel, leave at 3.50 p.m. and arrive in Berne by 8.22 p.m. In 1990, a TGV achieved a world train speed record travelling at 320.2mph (515.3km/h).

A feature of the early TGV trains was their long nose section, although more recent examples have a less angular front, the change improving the aerodynamic lines of the train within the context of a programme to improve overall efficiency that also witnessed the partial change from steel to aluminium alloy for the superstructure of the cars. Another key feature of the TGV is an electronic device that continuously monitors the line: whenever it senses a change, it adjusts the power input to the traction motors to maintain the speed set by the driver. First-class travellers on the TGV have all the benefits of luxurious semi-compartment seating, but second-class passengers also enjoy high-quality accommodation, and there are two areas of seating bays optimized for family groups as well as a play area and a nursery. In addition, there is special accommodation for the disabled.

Although the international design and manufacturing group responsible for the design of the *Eurostar* train used the same basic principles as found in the TGV, it also introduced a number of changes. The main difference between the *Eurostar* and the TGV is that the former, operating in several countries, had to be able to employ the electrical supply of three different systems, including current collection from a third rail in the U.K. and from overhead lines elsewhere. The resulting *Eurostar* design

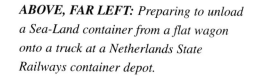

ABOVE, FAR LEFT: *Preparing to unload a Sea-Land container from a flat wagon onto a truck at a Netherlands State Railways container depot.*

ABOVE CENTRE LEFT: *Southern Pacific's triple-unit, double-stack railroad cars being loaded with containers. The articulated cars, built in three units over four sets of bogies, reduce the weight of rail equipment needed to carry containers by nearly one-half, compared with traditional single-level flatcars.*

ABOVE CENTRE RIGHT: *Trailers on Kangourou wagons of an SNCF specialist freight train, in the late 1970s.*

ABOVE: *Santa Fe Railroad's Ten-Pack unit awaiting loading of road trailers for its TOFC (Trailer On Flat Car) traffic at Hobart Yard, Los Angeles.*

LEFT: *Part of the display on the inaugural day of Channel Tunnel traffic from the Willesden Euroterminal, London.*

ABOVE: *A Santa Fe Railroad Six-Pack unit being loaded with truck trailers.*

ABOVE RIGHT: *Another scene on the inaugural day of Channel Tunnel traffic from Willesden Euroterminal, with a Railfreight Class 47 locomotive.*

RIGHT: *Engine 47375 about to leave with the second inaugural train from Euroterminal.*

has an exterior that was designed in the U.K. and an interior that was a collaborative Belgian and French undertaking. There were many mechanical and electrical problems that had to be solved in the design and manufacturing processes. The safety requirements of the Channel Tunnel, for example, require that passengers can be shifted from one end of the train to the other, and this fact made it impossible for the train to be designed as two sub-units merely connected in the middle. The *Eurostar* has two motor cars, these being located at the front and back of the 20-car set, and to offset to a limited extent the advantage in power enjoyed by two equivalent TGV sets, motorized bogies are used under the first and last passenger cars. Two other notable aspects of the design were the need for the overall size of the bogies to be reduced, and for a higher-extending pantograph to make contact with the higher overhead electric power lines installed in the Channel Tunnel. The need for the *Eurostar* to be fully compatible with the railroad arrangements of the three countries in which it was designed to operate dictated the creation of footsteps that automatically matched themselves to different platform heights, and the solution of problems associated with the various complex signalling systems used in Belgium, France, Germany and the U.K.

These and other aspects and problems were successfully negotiated and, to the great credit of the international design and manufacturing teams, the programme was fully completed between 1987 and 1994,

OPPOSITE
LEFT: *An SNCF TGV in Alsace during 1981. The TGV network required construction of completely new high-speed rail across the French countryside.*

RIGHT: *A* Eurostar *express from France, with power units 3225 and 3226, passing Wandsworth Road, London.*

when regular scheduled services were inaugurated during November.

Lying 377ft (115m) under mean sea level, the Channel Tunnel is a prodigious engineering feat and, at an overall length of 31.03 miles (49.93km), is the lengthiest underwater tunnel anywhere in the world. Passage through the Channel Tunnel by *Eurostar* takes about 20 minutes, and on emerging on the French side of the tunnel the *Eurostar* can accelerate to its highest permitted speed on the part of

the route connecting Calais with Paris.

The completion of the Tokaido section of Japan's Shinkansen railroad system in 1960 heralded a new era in rail transportation. For the previous 21 years the world record for the highest scheduled train speed had been held by Italy, which during July 1939 operated a three-car articulated set over the 195.8-mile (315.1-km) route linking Florence and Milan at an average speed of 102mph (164km/h). Japan's new railroad was designed for operations at

130mph (209km/h). Specially designed and constructed to permit operations at very high sustained speeds, this railroad features curves with a radius of no less than 2,185 yards (2000m), and though designed in an era before the concept of 'environmental friendliness' became so common as to become a truism, the line was conceived on the basis of carriage some 21ft (6.4m) above towns on viaducts with high side walls to avoid urban congestion and minimize noise. There are no level

crossings on the track, valleys and river estuaries are crossed on long viaducts, and wherever mountains blocked the intended way no less than 66 tunnels, of which 12 are more than 1.5miles (2.4km), were driven through the barrier.

As is the case with the TGV, the need to cater for the aerodynamic effect of two trains passing in opposite directions at a combined speed of more than 250mph (400km/h) had to be factored into the operational equation. As a result, the

distance between the nearest rails of opposing tracks in the tunnels was increased from the standard 6ft (1.8m) to a figure of between 9ft (2.7m) and 9ft 6in (2.89m).

During the later 1990s, a Hikari (lightning) train of the Shinkansen system departs Tokyo for Osaka every 15 minutes in the time period between 6.00 a.m. and 9 p.m., and the service covers the 322-mile (518-km) route in a mere 3 hours 10 minutes. Making only two halts, at Nagoya

and Kyoto, each 16-car train, carrying 1,000 passengers on average, travels at an average speed of over 100mph (160km/h). Despite the age of its design, reflecting the railroad technology of the 1960s rather than the 1990s, the Hikari is still an impressive train, but is now being replaced by the altogether more capable Nozomi 500, which entered revenue-earning service during March 1997. This unmistakable train makes one round trip between Osaka and Hakata daily as the fastest regularly

ABOVE: The 18.52 Waterloo to Paris Eurostar service, standing at Ashford station in Kent before diving into the Channel Tunnel.

ABOVE RIGHT: Power-cars 3005 and 3006 head west past Queen Street, east of Paddock Wood, Kent, operating the 12.31 Brussels to Waterloo train.

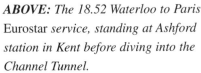

OPPOSITE: A British Rail HST 125 diesel-electric train.

scheduled train service in the world, and in the course of its journey travels at speeds of up to 186mph (300km/h).

In Russia, the core element of the Commonwealth of Independent States that emerged from the collapse of the U.S.S.R. in 1991, a publicly quoted company, High-Speed Railways, has undertaken with the Ministry of Railways of the Russian Federation the collaborative development of the Sokol as an electrically-powered high-speed train for the movement of passengers. Under consideration since 1987 as an alternative to the ER 200 concept of Soviet

times, and designed by the Central Construction Bureau of Marine Engineering, the train is built by Transmash at Tikhvin. Designed for ecologically-friendly operation, the Sokol is designed to carry more than 800 passengers, in both tourist and business classes, with speeds of between 155 and 217mph (250 and 350km/h). The train is 1,059ft (322.8m) long and has 12 cars, and was created to use two types of traction power in the form of 3,000-volt direct current and 25,000-volt alternating current delivered to 16 three-phase induction motors each rated at 905hp

(675kW) for a combined power of 14,485hp (10800kW). A refreshment car is standard, and other features of the Sokol are an international telephone capability and special accommodation for physically-handicapped passengers.

Intended primarily for service on the new specialized high-speed main line linking Moscow and St. Petersburg, the Sokol can also run at speeds up to 125mph (200km/h) on more conventional railroad lines. It is planned that 150 Sokol trains should be in full service by 2010, but of course the parlous state of the CIS's

OPPOSITE: *A Soviet ER 200 high-speed 14-coach electric passenger train.*

LEFT: *A suburban diesel multiple unit with a main-line electric locomotive in Moscow.*

economy makes it difficult to predict real progress. As work on the Sokol continues, special stations are being constructed to handle the trains: during July 1997, work started on the new terminal next to the Moscow Station in St. Petersburg and, at the other end of the line, the Riga Station in Moscow is also being remodelled.

Although trials with the operation of very-high-speed trains had been undertaken since 1903, it was to be more than 60 years before the potential of very-high-speed railroad transport for full public services, with services averaging more than 100mph (160km/h) start-to-stop but possessing a maximum operating speed of at least 130mph (209km/h), finally started to become a reality. The first of the new breed appeared in Japan in 1965 with the inauguration of the Japanese National

Railways' almost futuristic Shinkansen line from Tokyo westwards to Osaka. The line had been opened in 1964, but a preliminary period of operation at more normal speeds had been deemed prudent before full-speed services were introduced. Despite the impression they gave with their rocket-like lines for minimum drag, the Shinkansen ('new line') trains are in essence orthodox in their basic concept. The very high speed of these trains is attributable, therefore, not to any radical revision of train concepts but rather to the use of very high power: the standard 16-car Shinkansen has available to it for continuous running no less than 15,870hp (11840kW), and the train's notably high acceleration (a feature of vital importance in very fast start-to-stop speeds) is derived from the fact that every axle is powered.

The very high performance and the resultant extent of the great international fame gained by Japan with its Shinkansen trains thus served to disguise, if that is the right word, the capability that the Japanese engineers had extracted from existing railroad technology by the exercise of ingenuity in the creation of a 'clean sheet of paper' design. Up to 1964 the Japanese National Railways had used only the 42-in (1067-mm) gauge, but despite the additional cost involved, the organization secured authorization for the creation of a new line system that was wholly separate from the existing system, even to the extent of its gauge. The capital investment required for the construction of a completely new standard-gauge (56.5-in/1435-mm) track

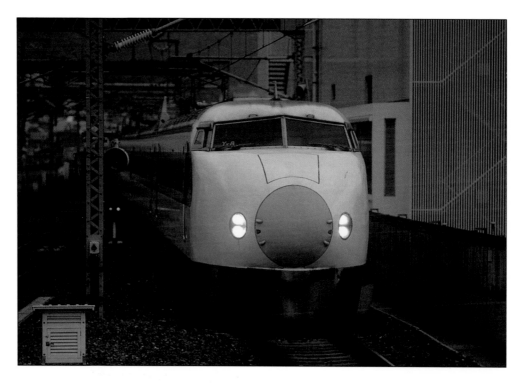

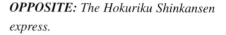

LEFT: The Shinkansen Kordanna *arriving at Kyoto, Japan in July 1995.*

BELOW: A Shinkansen (Nozomi) R-500 high-speed train set.

OPPOSITE: The Hokuriku Shinkansen express.

system to link some of Japan's most important cities was enormous, but the enthusiasm and far-sightedness of the men urging the undertaking was fully justified, not just in terms of the kudos gained for Japan, but also by the tripling of passenger ticket sales on the Shinkansen routes between 1966 and 1973.

The financial price of high-speed railroad operations to the Japanese was very large. For a start, land had to be bought at the escalating costs of the period for the construction of new railroad tracks into and out of the major urban centres, and at the same time the need to create track with the radius of any curve no less than 2,735 yards (2500m), to ensure the trains' safe negotiation of such curves, also required the

purchase of rural land. In addition to the purchase of the necessary land there was also the high cost of construction for track in a new gauge and to improved standards of accuracy, and also the inordinately high expense of boring tunnels through major obstacles to avoid bypassing these obstacles, which in the short term would have required additional land purchase and in the long term have reduced average speed by increasing the track length. However, one advantage that accrued from the powerful nature of the trains themselves was that comparatively steep gradients, up to 1/65, could be allowed.

So far as the trains themselves were concerned, the primary innovation was the self-signalling system that was introduced.

Both acceleration and deceleration are therefore not only automatic but in fact started automatically when required, on the final deceleration to a halt being wholly under the control of the driver. The Shinkansen system has no line-side signals, and all the important data concerning state-of-the-line are transmitted to the driver's cab by coded impulses sent along the main overhead power lines and passed onto the train by the pantograph. The automatic nature of the system is also reflected in the fact that the trains themselves transmit the signals required to set the route ahead of them wherever there is something to be selected. Another feature of the system, made necessary by the fact that Japan lies on a major fault line on the earth's crust and is therefore prone to volcanic activity, is the location of seismographs in the primary control centres, and these are linked into the system to generate automatic stop signals to all trains in the event that an earthquake is detected.

As the system was originally completed, there were 480 cars disposed in 40 sets each of 12 cars, each 12-car set being divided in electrical terms into six two-car units, one of which containing the buffet car, and with the highly streamlined ends and driving cabs (leading to the popular nickname 'bullet train' for the Shinkansen train) located at the front and back of the train. By 1970, however, the level of traffic and the fact that demand for the services was still increasing led to the decision to lengthen each train to 16 cars including two buffet cars. At much the same

time, the frequency of the services operated over the Shinkansen service was boosted from 120 to more than 200 per day in each direction, and this intensification of the service was made possible by the fact that there were now some 1,400 cars in service, these being used to constitute some 87 16-car sets.

In 1970, as soon as the technical and commercial success of the original system had become evident, the Japanese developed a plan to extend the Shinkansen network from the 320 miles (515km) of the original line to some 6,400 miles (10300km) to tie most of Japan's major cities into the system. The first stage of this process involved the 1,188 miles (1912km) of new track for the links between Tokyo and Okayama, Tokyo and Hakata, Oomiya (Tokyo) and Niigata, and Oomiya (Tokyo) and Morioka. The sheer volume of the work involved, especially in the mountain regions that the lines had to penetrate and in the 11.6-mile (18.6-km) undersea tunnel between two islands meant an enormous quantity of civil engineering work needed. The extent of this work is indicated by the fact that on the 247-mile (398-km) route between Okayama and Hakata, some 55 per cent of the track was laid in tunnels and 31 per cent on bridges or viaducts, meaning that only 14 per cent was laid as conventional railway on the ground. It should be borne in mind, however, that while much of the civil engineering task's size was attributable to the nature of the Japanese home islands with their masses of mountains and deep river valleys, part of it

was the result of the decision that was taken at this time to reduce gradients to a maximum of 1/65 and increase the maximum radius of curves to 4,375 yards (4000km) so that the maximum speed could be increased from 130mph (210km/h) to 162mph (260km/h). This maximum speed has not been fully realized in service, but even so the trains, operating on a hourly schedule, cover the 735-mile (1182-km) distance between Tokyo and Hakata at an average speed of 110mph (176.5km/h) in a time of 6 hours 40 minutes.

Considered in a different perspective, the Shinkansen type of service would cover the comparable distance in the United States, typically between New York and Chicago, in just half the current scheduled running time of 18 hours 30 minutes.

It is worth noting that the train sets built for service on the Hakata extension have provision for operation at a higher speed in the future: the power available was increased by some 48 per cent to 23,600hp (17595kW) and the additional weight of the relevant electrical equipment was offset by the construction of the car superstructures in light alloy rather than steel. The data for the 16-car sets operated on the Shinkansen routes for high-speed passenger service include propulsion by alternating 25,000-volt 50-Hz electrical current fed via overhead catenary and step-down transformers and rectifiers to 64 248-hp (185-kW) motors each driving an axle by means of gearing and flexible drive, total weight of 2,031,200lb (921352kg), overall length of 1,318ft 6in (401.880m) and

maximum speed of 130mph (210km/h).

The excellence of the train sets operated on the Shinkansen services may be judged from the performance and overall capabilities of contemporary American and European counterparts. In the United States, for example, there appeared during 1967 the Pennsylvania Railroad's Metroliner Two-Car Trainset. The origins of this type can be found in the generally low level of service provided to American passengers by the railroad companies during the 1960s. This reflected the fact that most railroads were operating passenger services only at a considerable financial deficit, and at the same time losing passengers to the airlines over long- and medium-distance routes, on which the airliner could offer an average speed perhaps 10 times higher than that of

ABOVE LEFT: The Seikan tunnel with main bore on the right, and works tunnel to the left. The tunnel provides a rail link between Honshu and the northern island of Hokkaido.

ABOVE: Japanese National Railways 130-mph (210-km/h) Shinkansen high-speed train.

OPPOSITE: One of Amtrak's Metroliners carrying passengers between major cities in the New York-Washington North-East Corridor.

the train, and to the private motor car for short-distance routes, in which potential passengers seemed increasingly to prefer the advantages of door-to-door transport even though there was no or, at best, only modest time advantage. Faced with this situation, which seemed likely to end with the cessation of virtually all passenger services, the American railroad operators decided that they could in fact compete with the motor car if they disposed of their fleets of wholly obsolescent passengers cars and adopted not only new cars but also a new 'go get 'em' marketing image.

One route that seemed eminently suitable for the treatment was the Pennsylvania Railroad's electrified main line between New York and Washington, D.C. via Philadelphia on what is now known as the North-East Corridor, and it was for this that there was designed and developed the Metroliner Two-Car Trainset. The Pennsylvania Railroad had bought the 'MP 85'-class prototypes of possible locomotive types from the Budd Company of Philadelphia as early as 1958, and during 1963 the city of Philadelphia purchased on behalf of the railroad some Budd Silverliner passenger cars. Later in the decade the railroad received a measure of U.S. federal government aid toward a $22 million scheme for the creation of new high-speed self-propelled trains, as well as $33 million toward the improvements required for the permanent way if operations at the planned maximum speed of 160mph (257km/h) were to become a reality.

Orders were placed in 1966 with Budd

for 50 (later increased to 61) stainless steel Metroliner cars. These were powered on all of their wheels, could attain considerably more than the specified speed and had the truly impressive short-term power/weight ratio of 34hp (25.35kW)/tonne. They also had a system for dynamic braking down to 30mph (48km/h), and also provision for

automatic speed control, acceleration and deceleration in the basis of new concepts, and other modern features of the cars were air-conditioning, airline-type catering, electrically-controlled doors, and even a public radio telephone service. The order included parlour cars and snack-bar coaches as well as ordinary day coaches. Each of

the cars had a driving cab at one end, but there was provision for access between adjacent cars when the cab was not in use. The cars were arranged on a semi-permanent basis in pairs as two-car units.

Reflecting enthusiasm rather than practical consideration and the step-by-step approach typical of the Pennsylvania

Railroad during its heyday, however, the decision was taken to order the type straight 'off the drawing board'. The result was the discovery of a catalogue of faults whose rectification several times delayed the new cars' entry into revenue-earning service. Pennsylvania Central took over the programme in 1958, and it was only in 1969 that the first limited services began, revealing the need for a modification programme (costing no less than 50 per cent of the original purchase price) before full public service could be considered.

In May 1971 the new Amtrak organization took over from Pennsylvania Central, and by the middle of 1972 the Metroliner was being used for some 14 daily services operated at a start-to-stop speed scheduled for a speed as high as 95mph (153km/h). Even so, speeds as high as the announced 150mph (241km/h) could not be achieved in public service, for the work that had been completed on the track was sufficient for a maximum speed of only 110mph (177km/h). A programme of track work was later implemented for the North-East Corridor: at a cost of $2.5 billion (75 times the originally estimated cost!) this included the track between New York and the Boston line. Only after the completion of this work was the originally envisaged speed feasible, but the Metroliners were now beginning to show their age and were replaced on the primary section of the route between New York and Washington by 'AEM7'-type locomotives hauling trains of Amfleet cars that are in effect unpowered Metroliners. This change meant the

relegation of the Metroliners to the route linking New York with Harrisburg via Philadelphia.

The original schedule of 2 hours 30 minutes for the service between New York and Washington was never managed, but the hourly services did manage the trip in 3 hours with four intermediate halts at an average speed of 75mph (120km/h). The data for the Metroliner Two-Car Trainset included propulsion by 11,000-volt 25-Hz alternating electrical current fed via overhead catenary, step-down transformer and rectifiers to eight 300-hp (224-kW) motors of which one was geared to each pair of wheels, total weight 328,400lb (148962kg), overall length of 170ft 0in (51.82m) and maximum theoretical speed of 160mph (257km/h).

Altogether greater success attended a number of pioneering European high-speed trains, of which perhaps the most successful of all was the British High Speed Train 125 introduced to service in 1978 as the fastest diesel-electric train anywhere in the world. The HST 125 was a considerable if belated step forward in British express passenger train history and, in the process, marked the first genuine success for the U.K.'s nationalized railway industry in the field of passenger transport. The key to this success was the decision, taken right at the beginning of the programme, not to attempt too much and therefore to limit the design team to well-established technology and thus minimize the risks associated with the use of novel technologies.

The HST 125 should therefore be

ABOVE: British Rail's High Speed Train was designed to produce significant decreases in journey times on non-electrified InterCity routes. The prototype train comprised two power coaches each containing a 2250-hp (1678-kW) diesel engine, five Mk III passenger coaches and two catering vehicles.

ABOVE RIGHT: A British Rail HST 125. The 125mph (200km/h) High Speed Train is an important technical advance based on the stretching of existing technology.

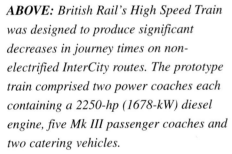

OPPOSITE: An Amtrak Metroliner in the North-East Corridor between Washington, D.C. and Boston.

regarded as a development, perhaps of a fairly extensive nature, of current thinking and even equipment with the possible exception of the bogie suspension. The most radical change in the HST 125 was associated with the type's operation, for instead of being an entirely separate unit that could be detached for the hauling of other types of train or for the type of frequent maintenance that was required with older generations of locomotive, the HST 125 locomotive was schemed within the context of a self-propelled and therefore fully integrated train of the fixed-formation type. This opened the realistic possibilities of speeds in the order of 125mph (201km/h) without problem and, as there was no need for provision for alternative use, of a much simplified locomotive

(without vacuum-brake equipment, slow-running equipment and the like) that would be lighter, cheaper to build and operate, and also require less maintenance.

It has to be admitted that self-propelled trains do possess a number of disadvantages, but also advantages such as the ability to reach a terminus and exit on the return service in a time as little as 20 minutes and, as a result of their lower weight and reduced complexity, the ability to cover up to 250,000 miles (402325km) per year with little likelihood of mechanical problems. Moreover, an important fact in the decision to adopt the HST 125 was that the shorter journey times for long-distance routes would have spin-off advantages such as a reduced demand for sleeper carriages, which were costly to purchase and operate

but generated little in the way of revenue.

It was originally decided that a fleet of 132 HST 125 trains would be built to allow British Railways to provide high-speed services over its primary non-electrified routes, most notably those linking London's Paddington and King's Cross stations with destinations in the west of England, southern Wales, Yorkshire, north-east England, and Scottish cities such as Edinburgh and Aberdeen; and also north-east to south-west diagonal services in England via Sheffield, Derby and Birmingham. The plan was then to reduce the number of HST 125 trains to 95 as a means of generating a comprehensive schedule of high-speed services unmatched elsewhere in the world at the time.

The shortening of the scheduled service

LEFT: *An HST 125 with a rake of nine coaches in a winter setting.*

OPPOSITE
ABOVE LEFT: *The arrangement of the power car for the HST 125.*

ABOVE RIGHT: *An InterCity 125 crossing the world-famous Forth Bridge during its journey from King's Cross, London to Aberdeen, Scotland.*

BELOW: *An InterCity 125, setting out from the 'Granite City', Aberdeen, at the start of its run to London.*

time made possible by the use of the HST 125 on routes allowing the maximum speed to be maintained for some time was considerable, which translated into a 20 per cent reduction in the time required for many services: for example, the route between King's Cross and Newcastle could be covered in as little as 2 hours 54 minutes by comparison with the 3 hours 35 minutes required for services hauled by 'Deltic'-class diesel locomotives. The advent of the HST 125 was clearly approved by the travelling public, which appreciated not only the reduction in journey times but also the improvement in the level of comfort provided by the HST 125's specially designed cars.

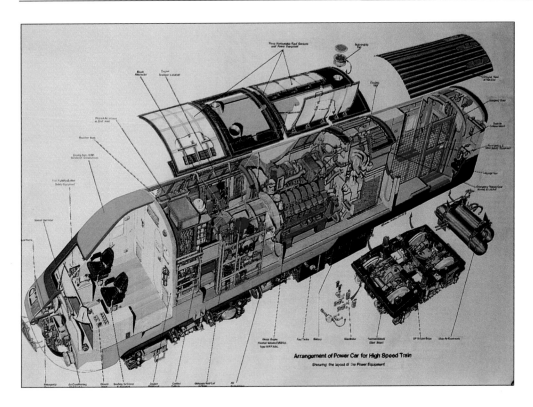

Arrangement of Power Car for High Speed Train
Showing the layout of the Power Equipment

In mechanical terms, the design of the HST 125's locomotive was based on the use of one 2,260-hp (1685-kW) Paxman Valenta lightweight diesel engine installed in each of the motor/baggage carriages at each end of the train. The specific power of the engines was about double that of the standard diesel engines used in others of British Railways' classes of locomotive, and the engines were also notably compact. These two aspects of the powerplant meant that the motor/baggage car could be designed within a weight limit of 154,000lb (69854kg), and that it was also possible to allocate volume in the rear of each unit's overall length of 58ft 4in (17.792m) for baggage and the guard's accommodation. It was also appreciated from the beginning of the programme that the low axle-loads of the HST 125 trains would have a beneficial effect on the longevity of the tracks over which they operated.

The HST 125's Mk III carriages resulted from 10 years of development from the Mk I type that had been standard since the 1950s and, despite the addition of features such as air-conditioning, sound-proofing, advanced bogies, automatic corridor doors and a level of comfort hitherto unprecedented for second-class passengers, there was a 40 per cent reduction in weight per seat, this being partially attributable to the adoption of open-plan rather than compartmented

OPPOSITE: An HST 125 on the East Coast Main Line. By the mid-1990s these locomotives were being transferred to the other express lines.

RIGHT: The prototype 125-mph (200-km/h) HST of British Rail during trials on the East Coast Main Line. The world speed record of diesel traction was achieved during these trials when the HST reached 141mph (227km/h) on 11 June 1973.

BELOW RIGHT: The interior of the second-class saloon coach of British Rail's HST 125.

accommodation, and partially to an increase in length from some 64ft (19.51m) to 75ft 6in (23.01m) for an extra two seating bays. A feature of the HST 125's operation that especially appealed to passengers was the very smooth ride afforded at high speed even over indifferent track. This was the result of the use of some aspects of the air suspension developed for the APT. Including refreshment vehicles, the HST 125 trains generally had seven or eight passenger cars for nine- or 10-carriage sets with a power/baggage carriage at each end.

The avowed object of the HST 125 was the provision of a superior service on existing track without the additional cost of what would have been involved in electrification or even the most limited of reconstruction and modification efforts. This concept meant that the HST 125, despite its higher speed, had to be able to halt when required at signals within the warning distances inherent in the current generation of signalling equipment: for this reason the braking system included disc brakes on all the wheels and an advanced wheel-slip correction capability.

British Railways proceeded via the construction and evaluation of a complete HST 125 train set. This, on occasion, reached speeds as high as 143mph (230km/h), which represented a world record for diesel traction. Even though the performance of the HST 125 was

ABOVE LEFT: *Germany's ICE (InterCity Express) railroad service is one of the three types of train operating on Germany's extensive railroad network for long-distance services between distant termini with few intermediate halts, and offers an attractive combination of comfort and speed of 174mph (280km/h).*

ABOVE: *The IR (InterRegio) is the slowest of the three elements constituting that operated by the German railroad network, and was designed for the creation of quick connections between cities and country areas at speeds of 124mph (200km/h).*

LEFT: *Britain's HST 125.*

OPPOSITE: *The LRC (Light, Rapid and Comfortable) train prototype during tests in Canada in 1978. The LRC incorporates automatic body-tilting.*

impressive, however, there was a number of individually small but cumulatively annoying minor problems as the first production trains entered service. These problems were quickly solved, however, and a factor that particularly endeared the HST 125 to passengers at this time was the fact that the failure of one power/baggage carriage did not immobilize the whole train and the power/baggage car at the other end was sufficient to move the train, albeit at a slower but still useful speed. The data for the HST 125 in its 10-carriage set included the powerplant of two 2,250-hp (1678-kW) Paxman Valenta 12RP200L diesel engines, each possessing an integral alternator delivering electrical current to the four motors in the bogie frames, total weight of 844,132lb (382898kg), overall length of 720ft 5in (219.58m) and maximum speed of 125mph (200km/h).

A slightly later contemporary of British Railways' HST 125 was the Deutsche

The evaluation of this all-electric conversion persuaded the Deutsche Bundesbahn to place a contract for five eight-wheel locomotives based dynamically on the experimental conversion, and these units appeared in 1979. The specification called for the locomotives to haul passenger trains of 700 tonnes at 99mph (160km/h), fast freight trains of 1,500 tonnes at 62mph (100km/h), and heavy freight trains of 2,700 tonnes at 50mph (80km/h): despite its weight of 185,185lb (84000kg), the locomotives achieved these tasks without problem. Full advantage was taken of the good adhesion of the induction motors, with a continuous rating of 7,510hp (5600kW), making the units the most powerful four-axle locomotives anywhere in the world.

Initial evaluation discovered several problems as well as revealing the overall capabilities of the locomotives, but once these difficulties had been not so much cured as brought under control, the locomotives were tested on a number of types and weights of train, and one of them was also subjected to high-speed trials hauling one test coach. This combination touched 143.5mph (231km/h), thus beating the previous world record for traction by induction motor, established in 1903 in the Zossen-Marienfelde trials in Germany with high-speed motor coaches. Another impressive achievement was an acceleration from stationary to 124mph (200km/h) in just 30 seconds. One of the locomotives was later evaluated on the Lötschberg route in Switzerland where, in severe weather conditions, it proved almost as effective on

a 1/37 gradient as a lower-speed locomotive designed specifically for such tasks.

These results and later were decidedly encouraging, but the Deutsche Bundesbahn has yet to decide whether or not to exploit the manifest capabilities of such three-phase traction, which is notably expensive. What cannot be denied, however, is that the induction motor is the most promising new development in electric traction, and could well become less expensive if it enters production to the stage at which economies of scale become significant The data for the 120-class locomotive include propulsion by 15,000-volt 16.67-Hz alternating current from overhead wires rectified by thyristors and then inverted by thyristors to variable-frequency three-phase alternating current for supply to four 1,878-hp (1400-kW) induction traction motors with spring drive, tractive effort 76,435lb (34670kg), total weight 185,185lb (84000kg), overall length 63ft 0in (19.200m) and maximum speed of 99mph (160km/h).

Given the bi-lingual official nature of Canada, the LRC Bo-Bo locomotive uses as its designation an acronym that was specially selected to be the same in both English and French: LRC stands for Light, Rapid and Comfortable in English and Lèger, Rapide et Confortable in French. What is also evident, however, is that the L could also stand for Lourd (heavy), for the LRC passenger car turns the scales at some 57 per cent more than the same-capacity equivalent hauled by the British HST 125 motor/baggage carriage, which is itself 20 per cent lighter than the LRC's locomotive.

Bundesbahn's '120' class of Bo-Bo electric locomotives intended for more flexible operation at moderately high speeds on mixed-traffic routes. There are three types of electric motor (direct current, one-phase alternating current and three-phase alternating current), and the characteristics of each type were already well understood by the beginning of the 20th century. Despite the availability and nature of the three types of electric motor, the choice between them was generally governed by the preferred method of power supply and control rather than any specific motor quality. The direct current and one-phase alternating current commutator motors proved to be the most adaptable of the types to the control equipment then available, and as a consequence three-phase alternating current motors were little used. In more modern times, however, technical developments have made the three-phase alternating current motor a more practical

item: the two types of three-phase electric motor are the synchronous type, in which the frequency is connected directly to the supply frequency, and asynchronous or induction type. The latter has first-class traction features, and after a number of European experimental installations of induction motors during the 1960s and 1970s for both diesel-electric and electric locomotives, the Henschel company of West Germany built during 1971 three private-venture diesel locomotives with 2,500-hp (1864-kW) engines powering induction motors, using an electrical system produced by Brown Boveri. The Deutsche Bundesbahn bought these locomotives, which were tested exhaustively and then placed in full service. During 1974 one of the locomotives was stripped of its diesel engine, ballast being added to keep the locomotive's weight unaltered, and the locomotive was coupled permanently to a pantograph-equipped electric test coach.

These weight factors aside, the LRC is a significant offering in the high-speed train stakes, its capabilities tarnished only moderately by the number of failures it had encountered during a number of early efforts to get the type into full service before all its teething problems had been eliminated.

The LRC entered service in 1981 on the route linking Toronto and Montreal, a 337-mile (542-km) journey for which a time of 3 hours 40 minutes was initially scheduled for a 45-minute saving over the schedule of the 'Turbo-train' used on the route since the late 1970s. By July 1982 the schedule timed had been extended to 4 hours 25 minutes, the same as that of the Turbo-train, with the caveat that the schedule was also subject to alterations that might result in a delay of almost one hour. This was a reflection of the fact that during the previous winter there had been major problems with powdery snow getting into the locomotives' advanced internal equipment and causing havoc.

Despite these and other problems, there is no doubt that the LRC is essentially of capable concept that was not pushed into service until a 14-year development period had been completed. The most interesting feature incorporated in the LRC is provision for a tilt of up to 8.5° to improve safety and passenger comfort as the train passes round curves at high speed. This tilting capability is restricted to the passengers cars as it was thought unnecessary and also expensive for incorporation in the locomotive, which carries a large diesel engine providing

ABOVE and OPPOSITE: *The LRC type of train was designed and built to provide moderately fast and comfortable passenger railroad services in Canada's more heavily populated areas. However, in service, it was soon found to be compromised by the weight of the locomotives and passenger cars, resulting in trains whose poor power/weight ratio adversely affected the type's operating economics and, as a result of the need to cruise at high power settings in an effort to maintain an adequately fast schedule, mechanical reliability that was far inferior to that originally specified. Another problem was the fact that development and introduction of the equipment was also inordinately protracted.*

power for traction and also for the considerable demands of the air-conditioning and heating systems necessary for passenger comfort in the excesses of the Canadian summer and winter. The initial order covered 22 locomotives and 50 passenger cars for service with VIA Rail Canada, but problems with the passenger cars' most advanced feature, the tilting system, meant that in the short term there were too many locomotives for the number of carriages available, and the surplus was used to haul other trains, for example the *International Limited* between Toronto and Chicago in the northern U.S.A.

The data for the LRC locomotive include propulsion by one 3,900-hp (2908-kW) Alco Type 251 diesel engine powering an alternator feeding (via rectifiers) four direct-current traction motors geared to the axles, total weight of 185,185lb (84000kg), overall length of 66ft 5in (20.24m) and maximum theoretical speed of 125mph (201km/h) limited by general track conditions to 80mph (129km/h).

Such was the success of the British HST 125 that there were major hopes that other railroad operators might adopt it. As events turned out, the only country to evince any significant interest was Australia, in the form of the railway administration of the New South Wales Public Transport Administration. However, the version adopted in New South Wales as the XPT (Express Passenger Train) has a number of differences from the British original to reflect the somewhat different

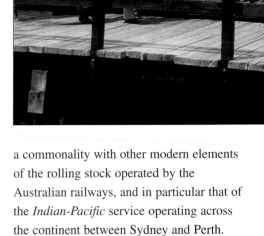

operating conditions of this Australian state. Most notably, the XPT is an eight-car train and therefore shorter than its British counterpart with two motor/baggage cars and between seven and nine passenger cars. Although the Paxman diesel engines of the XPT are rated at something like 10 per cent less than those in the British motor/baggage car, increasing their life and improving fuel economy to marked extents, the lower weight of the shorter train gives the XPT a higher power/weight ratio, and in combination with lower gearing (itself a reflection of the fact that Australian track alignments are incapable of supporting

speeds in the order of 125mph/200km/h) this produces significantly higher acceleration, and this improves the overall performance of the train on services with numerous stops and slow sections. Another change was effected in the bogies, for early evaluation of the HST 125 revealed that the original British pattern was not ideally suited to the tracks typical of Australian operations. Less obvious modifications were made to the ventilation system so that it could cope more effectively with the greater heat and dustiness of Australian service, and the passenger cars were manufactured from stainless steel to provide

a commonality with other modern elements of the rolling stock operated by the Australian railways, and in particular that of the *Indian-Pacific* service operating across the continent between Sydney and Perth.

The XPT entered full service in 1982, having first put paid to the criticisms of a not inconsiderable number of detractors by recording an Australian rail speed record of 144mph (231km/h) near Wagga-Wagga during August 1981. The XPT's first scheduled services were three daily routes operated out of Sydney, and a reflection of the capabilities of the new type was provided by a time saving of 1 hour

46 minutes for the 315-mile (506-km) route linking Sydney and Kempsey. The original Australian order was for 10 motor/baggage cars and 20 passengers cars, enough for four seven-car trains and a reserve of two motor/baggage cars, but the success of the new type was such that in April 1982 there followed an additional order for four motor/baggage cars and 16 passenger cars to create six eight-car trains reflecting the increased traffic on the routes operated by the XPT. Further proof of the success of the XPT had already been provided in February 1982 by the decision of the Victorian Railways to contract for sufficient rolling

RIGHT: A pre-production TGV running on existing track in Alsace, France during trials in 1979.

OPPOSITE: The introduction of the TGV on France's railroad network was preceded by a considerable quantity of infrastructure work to provide the right type of tracks and routes for these high-speed trains, and the subsequent extension of the TGV network meant additional work. That the French had planned correctly, however, is indicated by the fact that the TGV network operates at a profit.

stock to create three trains for the service linking Melbourne and Sydney.

The data for the XPT high-speed diesel-electric passenger train include propulsion by one 2,000-hp (1491-kW) Paxman Valenta diesel engine and alternator supplying direct current via solid-state rectifiers to four traction motors geared to the axles with hollow-axle flexible drive, a total weight of 826,500lb (374900kg), overall length of 590ft 2in (179.88m) and maximum speed of 100mph (161km/h).

The Soviet counterpart to the HST 125 was created as the ER 200, and this was planned as a 14-car train whose greater size reflected the generally larger passenger loads carried by Soviet train services in a country in which private car ownership and air travel were both severely restricted. The ER 200 was the Soviet railroad organization's first high-speed electric train of the self-propelled type, and was first

built in 1975 at the Riga Carriage Works in what is now the independent country of Latvia in the centre of the three Baltic states. The authorities' plan was to create a train capable of offering a genuinely high-speed service on the 406-mile (650-km) route connecting Moscow and Leningrad, the two most important cities of the U.S.S.R. The route is essentially straight, so the new train needed nothing like a tilting mechanism to ensure safety and comfort on curves of comparatively short radius, but only the power output needed to accelerate the train to a high cruising speed and then maintain it at that basic level, and the brakes to decelerate the train safely. The power output selected for the task was some 13,840hp (10320kW), and the chosen braking system combined electro-mechanical disc brakes for speeds below 22mph (35mph) and rheostatic brakes for speeds above 22mph; an electromagnetic rail brake was added for emergency use.

In electrical terms the train's 14 cars comprised six two-car powered units, each with 128 seats, and at each end an unpowered cab/passenger/baggage car with seating for 24 passengers, a small buffet section and baggage accommodation. A number of modern systems were designed for the new train, these systems including an 'autodriver' to respond automatically to transponder units located at track level to set the speed desired between particular points. It was reported that the ER 200 completed the journey between Moscow and Leningrad in 3 hours 5 minutes at an average speed of 106mph (170km/h) during

a 1980 test run, but entry into public service at anything like these speeds has not yet taken place. The data for the ER 200 high-speed electric train included propulsion by 3,000-volt direct current delivered via an overhead catenary to 48 288-hp (215-kW) traction motors driving the axles of the 12 intermediate cars by means of gearing and flexible drives, total weight of 1,829,806lb (830000kg), overall length of 1,220ft 6in (372.00m) and maximum speed of 124mph (200km/h).

There can be little doubt that the most impressive high-speed train in large-scale service anywhere in the world at the end of the 20th century is the TGV (Train Grande Vitesse, or high-speed train) operated by the French national railways, more properly known as the Société Nationale des Chemins de Fer. The origins of this type can be discerned as far back as 1955, when two French electric locomotives separately established a world train speed record of 205.7mph (331km/h) while undertaking tests designed to provide data on the design of the locomotive and the track that was required for very high-speed running. At the time, this might have been regarded as little more than experimental work, and as such not in any way bearing a practical relationship to the everyday world of railroad operations, which was currently limited in France to a maximum speed of only 87mph (140km/h). The lie was put to this impression by the fact that just 21 years later two prototype examples of a new French train intended for full service and not just trial work had on almost 225

ABOVE LEFT and RIGHT: *Work in progress on the Digoin railway project in France, in 1978. This was part of the very considerable effort that the French had to make to ensure that the system had the right combination of tracks and routes for the TGV.*

RIGHT: *A track inspection coach, capable of measuring the quality of track at 125mph, running behind the power car of a High Speed Train in the mid-1970s.*

OPPOSITE: *A prototype of an SNCF TGV during trials in the late 1970s. From the beginning of the prototype trials, it was clear that at the mechanical level, the TGV was clearly on the verge of considerable success.*

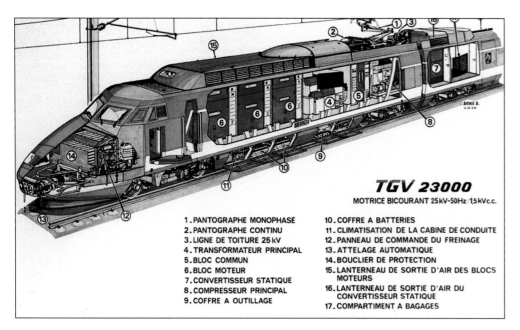

LEFT: This cutaway illustration reveals the interior of the first generation of TGV power cars with their powerful electric motors and, below a pantograph assembly, the associated transformers and converters.

BELOW: The trials of the TGV in the 1970s and early 1980s were marked by the establishment of a series of world speed records.

TGV 23000
MOTRICE BICOURANT 25kV-50Hz/1,5kVc.c.

1. PANTOGRAPHE MONOPHASE
2. PANTOGRAPHE CONTINU
3. LIGNE DE TOITURE 25 kV
4. TRANSFORMATEUR PRINCIPAL
5. BLOC COMMUN
6. BLOC MOTEUR
7. CONVERTISSEUR STATIQUE
8. COMPRESSEUR PRINCIPAL
9. COFFRE A OUTILLAGE

10. COFFRE A BATTERIES
11. CLIMATISATION DE LA CABINE DE CONDUITE
12. PANNEAU DE COMMANDE DU FREINAGE
13. ATTELAGE AUTOMATIQUE
14. BOUCLIER DE PROTECTION
15. LANTERNEAU DE SORTIE D'AIR DES BLOCS MOTEURS
16. LANTERNEAU DE SORTIE D'AIR DU CONVERTISSEUR STATIQUE
17. COMPARTIMENT A BAGAGES

The main problem was the conflicting requirement of fast passenger trains and considerably slower freight trains operating over the same tracks, which made the creation of scheduling that was both safe and efficient very difficult. As a result, the flow of traffic along the route was arranged in so-called 'flights', with passenger trains and freight trains scheduled in batches for movement at different times of the day. This system was at best a palliative, and there was thus a very strong argument for the creation of additional capacity. The start of work on the evaluation of the various ways in which this extra capacity could be provided started in 1966, and by this time it

times recorded a speed in exceed of 186mph (300km/h).

Just as significantly, the French railway organization had already started work on 236miles (380km) of new track designed to allow trains to run at these speeds on the route linking Paris and Lyons, the latter the central station in the route between Paris and Marseilles that had been the primary route of the old Paris, Lyons & Marseilles railroad company as it linked France's three most populous cities. As a result, the route was the location of the railroad company's heaviest traffic in the period leading up to World War II, and this factor increased after the end of the war as France was rebuilt. Electrification of the line in the period after the war improved the quality and reliability of the service, but also added additional passenger traffic, and by the 1960s the route was decidedly congested.

had already been decided that the new track would serve not only to reduce the pressure on the existing track, but also to allow the operation of more advanced trains at very much higher speeds than had hitherto been possible, in the process drawing passengers from the parallel road and air services, relieving pressure on these already overtaxed routes.

One fact that was evident from the beginning of the study was that the dedication of the new line to passengers rather than mixed traffic would offer significant construction and speed advantages as it would remove the need for the cambering of curves at the compromise (and therefore not optimized) angle required to cope with all speeds and weights of traffic. The new track was therefore conceived for the very much higher speeds that would be typical of the new trains operating only with passengers. The axle loads of freight vehicles can reach 44,092lb (20000kg) and those of electric locomotives 50,705lb (23000kg), but it was soon seen that if the axle loading of trains operating on the new line could be limited to a figure in the order of 37,478lb (17000kg) this would facilitate the maintenance of the track in a condition fully suitable for the operation of trains running at very high speed.

Drawing on the experience of the 1955 high-speed test operations, the French railway organization was able in 1967 to begin limited operations at speeds of up to 124mph (200km/h) on the route connecting Paris and Bordeaux on the south-west

LEFT and BELOW: Though not as advanced in purely aerodynamic terms as some of the high-speed trains that followed its pioneering lead, the TGV is still notably 'clean' in its exterior lines, and the avoidance of complex two- and three-dimensional curvatures also helped to keep manufacturing costs under control. This last fact was important as the creation of the required infrastructure was so expensive.

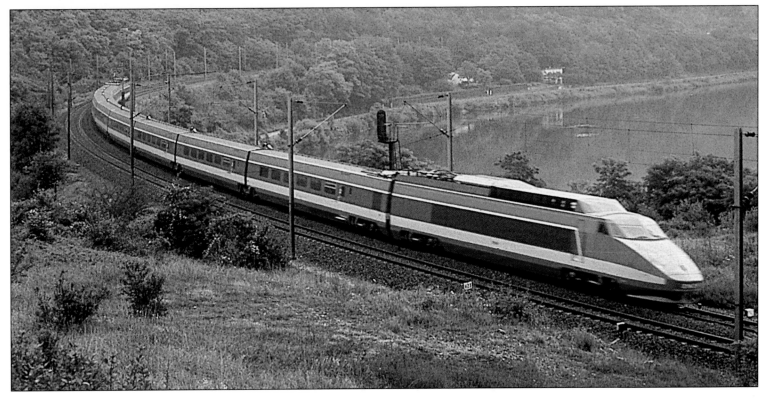

LEFT: Trolley service aboard Eurostar, Rail Europe.

OPPOSITE
ABOVE LEFT: First-class dining aboard Thalys, *Rail Europe.*

ABOVE RIGHT: A first-class meal aboard Eurostar.

BELOW LEFT: The upper-storey bar of a TGV Duplex double-decker.

BELOW RIGHT: The bar aboard Thalys, *Rail Europe.*

region of the country's railroad network. The same region was also used for further evaluation of high-speed running by special sets of railcars: the first experimental set with gas turbine power was run at speeds up to 147mph (236km/h), and one of the production sets with the same type of powerplant completed 10 runs at speeds of more than 155mph (250km/h). It was the initial experimental set with gas turbine propulsion for very high speeds that

indicated the way forward, however, and this TGV001 (later redesignated as the TGS so that the TGV appellation could be used for the parallel version with electric propulsion) became the first French train to be designed for running at a speed of 186mph (300km/h): the TVG001/TGS completed 175 runs in which it exceeded a speed of 186mph and also recorded a maximum speed of 197mph (317km/h). There was also built a special high-speed

electric motor coach that reached a maximum speed of 192mph (309km/h), clearly indicating that the French railroad organization was pushing forward the frontier of train performance right across the board of available technologies.

It was originally planned that the new track between Paris and Lyons should be used for high-speed passenger services based on trains using the technology pioneered and proved in the TVG001/TGS

experimental set. The cost of buying the land and then undertaking the considerable task of demolishing existing buildings and then building the new track within the built-up area of Paris was deemed too great for serious contemplation, so the new track was based on the use of the first 18.6 miles (30km) of existing track south from the Gare de Lyon, and therefore only a limited running speed, to the point at which the new track diverged from the existing

RIGHT: A TGV Duplex of Rail Europe.

BELOW LEFT: The Thalys 2 *service on the important route linking Paris and Amsterdam in the Netherlands.*

BELOW RIGHT: The Thalys 2 *service operates with the latest generation of locomotives, the* Eurostar *type.*

OPPOSITE: A unit of the latest generation of TGV trains, the TGV-R, cruises through northern France in the region of Lens.

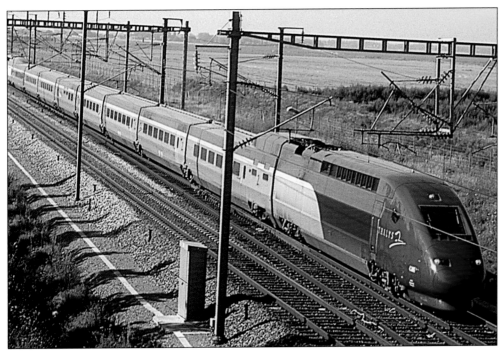

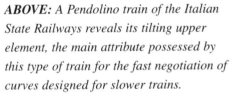

ABOVE: *A Pendolino train of the Italian State Railways reveals its tilting upper element, the main attribute possessed by this type of train for the fast negotiation of curves designed for slower trains.*

ABOVE RIGHT: *An Italian State Railways Settobello.*

OPPOSITE: *A Rail Europe TGV at speed.*

network for the main length of the run to Lyons at very much higher speed. The new track was linked with the existing network at two other places to provide a link for services to Dijon and to the Swiss cities of Lausanne and Geneva. The whole task required a very considerable injection of money from the French government for the capital investment in the new infrastructure, but the current financial strength of the services between Paris and Lyons meant that those planning the new service were not being fanciful when they predicted a considerable and comparatively rapid return on the capital investment.

Planning was well under way and final

government approval of the new system was imminent when a radical change was imposed by the financial problems that started to affect the Western world late in 1973 after the Arab nations that were the world's main sources of oil decided to raise their prices dramatically in an effort to use the 'oil weapon' as a means of reducing Western support for Israel, which had just achieved a major military success against Egypt and Syria in the Yom Kippur War of October 1973. Gas turbine propulsion for the TGV was therefore abandoned in favour of electric propulsion using overhead lines delivering 25,000 volts at 50Hz. Final planning for the route, and the revision of

the TGV for electric propulsion was being undertaken, taking into account the fact that only very fast passenger trains would be using the new route, which meant that gradients of hitherto impossible steepness could be used as the trains would have the kinetic energy to climb such gradients without major loss of speed: it was felt that so great would be this kinetic energy, which is the product of the train's mass and the square of its velocity, that gradients of 1/28.5, four times steeper than those of the current tracks, could be employed. The reduction in the amount of diversion and levelling required to establish the current type of flatter route meant a saving of about

ABOVE: *The Italian railroad system's Fiat Ferroviaria ETR 450 trains offer considerable air-conditioned comfort.*

LEFT: *The network covered by the ETR 450 service extends from Salerno, just below Naples, in the south via Rome and Florence to Bologna in the north, where the network bifurcates north-east to Padua and Venice, and north-west to Milan and Turin.*

OPPOSITE: *Like most other high-speed trains of the present generation, the ETR 401 or Pendolino train is electrically powered by current delivered from an overhead line by a pantograph arrangement.*

30 per cent in construction cost and also reduced the time required to build the new tracks. The longest gradient on the new line is such that the speed of the TGV is reduced from 162mph (260km/h) at the bottom to 137mph (220km/h) at the top, this 25-mph (40-km/h) loss of speed being quickly recovered once the train has reached level ground once more.

The initial order for the all-electric TGV was made in 1976, and delivery began in 1978. The basic structural and aerodynamic design of the TGS was carried over to the TGV but the propulsion arrangement was, of course, entirely different and for obvious cost and reliability reasons made use of existing components wherever possible. Each of the TGV trains is a 10-car set in the form of two motor cars and an articulated assembly of eight passenger cars with the adjacent ends of two cars carried by a common bogie. The available power is 8,450hp (6300kW), and this is transmitted to 12 motorized axles in the form of the four axles of each of the two motor cars and the two adjacent axles of the end bogies of the passenger cars at each end of the articulated set of cars. A useful feature of the electric propulsion arrangement is the fact that it can also be operated on the 1,500-volt direct current system used on the previously electrified elements of the French railroad system, while six of the train sets are also equipped to operate on the 15,000-volt 16.67-Hz power of the Swiss railroad system. For alternating current operation there is a transformer in each motor car.

The TGV train sets are based on a development of the type of bogie developed initially for the TGV001/TGS, and as the new lines are restricted in terms of their use to only the TGVs, the camber of the tracks on the curves is optimized for these train sets, which therefore require no tilting mechanism. The electric traction motors are mounted on the body of the motor car, and a flexible drive arrangement is used to transfer the motive power to the axles. By this means, the unsprung mass of the bogie is very low, and this is one of the reasons that the forces imposed on the track at 186mph (300km/h) are less than those of a standard electric locomotive moving at 124mph (200km/h).

The new TGV lines have no trackside signalling arrangements, for the driver receives signal indications in the cab. The maximum speed permitted on any section of the track is shown on a display in front of the driver, who thus sets the controller to the speed indicated, the control system then maintaining this speed on an automatic basis. The TGV has three braking systems, all of them controlled by the single driver's brake valve. These systems are of the dynamic, disc and wheel tread types. The dynamic system makes use of the electric traction motors as generators, feeding energy into resistances, and in the course of braking the motors are excited from a battery, so that failure of the overhead supply does not affect the braking: the dynamic braking system is effective from maximum speed to 1.9mph (3km/h). In normal service, the disc brakes are applied

to half their maximum braking capacity and wheel tread brakes are used only lightly to clean the wheel treads, but under emergency conditions all three systems are used fully for maximum deceleration effect, and the braking distance from 162mph (260km/h) is 3,825 yards (3500m).

Most of the 87 TGV train sets were completed with both first- and second-class accommodation, but six were delivered with only first-class accommodation and another three for the carriage of mail rather than passengers. The train sets were built by the Alsthom company, which undertook the manufacture of the motor cars and the passenger cars at Belfort and La Rochelle respectively. The vital initial testing and evaluation of the TGV in its production form was undertaken on the existing route between Strasbourg and Belfort, which is sufficiently straight that a sustained speed of 162mph (260km/h) was feasible, but as soon as the first part of the new line had been completed the rest of the test and evaluation effort was transferred to this location, and one of the train sets was modified with enlarged wheels to allow tests above the normal maximum speed: in February 1981 this train set established a new world train speed record of 236mph (380km/h).

Scheduled passenger services on the southern section of the new line were inaugurated during the course of September 1981, and the success of the new service's speed and comfort was soon attested by a 70 per cent increase in passenger loads. The northern section of the route between Paris

and Lyons opened for service late in 1983, allowing the inauguration of a scheduled service in the time of 2 hours for the 266-mile (428-km) route at the average speed of 134mph (215km/h), although the 1983 raising of the maximum permissible speed from 162 to 168mph (260 to 270km/h) allowed a slight reduction in time and thus a modest increase in average speed. Apart from a small number of teething problems, including modest damage to the overhead power lines at maximum speed, the TGV has operated with commendable efficiency and reliability from the start of its operational career. The ride on the new lines is excellent, although a degradation of comfort is evident when the TGV operates on older lines.

The success of the TGV led to a comparatively modest but steady expansion of its route network, and the data for the TGV high-speed articulated multiple-unit electric train includes propulsion by 1,500-, 15,000- or 25,000-volt direct current delivered from overhead wires and passed via rectifiers and/or chopper control to six 704-hp (525-kW) traction motors at each end of the train set and powers the axles by means of spring drives, total weight 841,711lb (381800kg), overall length 656ft 9.5in (200.19m) and maximum speed 162mph (260km/h) as the type entered service but later increased to 186mph (300km/h).

The Italian counterpart of the TGV, although to a smaller size and of slightly lower performance, is the ETR 401 Pendolino four-car train, which was the

ABOVE: *The ETR 401 Pendolino express at Orvieto station on the line between Rome and Florence.*

world's second class of tilting trains to enter service after the much slower Japanese '381'-class train that entered service in the mid-1970s. The ETR 401 resulted from a project financed by the Italian industrial giant Fiat, and the type is able to provide high speed by the combination of moderately good streamlining and the high power/weight ratio resulting from the use of an abundance of power in a comparatively light train. Adequate stopping power is offered by the incorporation of three separate braking systems: the standard system is dynamic braking, using the motors as dynamos, for low-speed use there is a system of conventional electro-pneumatic air brakes, and finally there is an electro-magnetic rail brake that, by its very nature, is wholly independent of the wheels and their adhesion to the track. Unlike the

OPPOSITE: *The ETR 401 Pendolino express leaves a tunnel on its way from Florence and Rome.*

the possibility of a reduction of 45 minutes by comparison with the standard scheduled time of 3 hours, a saving of some 25 per cent, but the operator sensibly opted not to press the matter to the limit and therefore scheduled the service for a time saving of some 20 minutes. The acceptance of the ETR 401 has gradually extended to other routes in Italy, but the type's somewhat chequered operational record has meant that there are still doubts about the system, which had been exported to Spain in the form of the so-called 'Basculante' trains.

The data for the ETR 401 Pendolino high-speed electric train with a body-tilting system include electric propulsion by 3,000-volt direct current from an overhead catenary to eight 335-hp (250-kW) motors (two to each car), each driving a single axle by means of cardan shafts and gearing, total weight of 354,938lb (161000kg), overall length of 340ft 2.5in (103.70m) and maximum speed of 156mph (250km/h).

An extremely ambitious concept that was ultimately cancelled as a failure because of its complex tilting system, the '370' class or 'APT' (Advanced Passenger Train) was intended to provide British Railways with an extremely capable train for service well into the 21st century. The origins of the APT-P can be found in the 1960s when British Railways entrusted its much-enlarged Research Department at Derby with the task of undertaking a complete study of one of the railroad's most basic problems, namely the rising of a flanged wheel over a railed track. From the

results of this study there appeared the technical feasibility for the design of a train, albeit still with flanged wheels, offering the possibility of very smooth running at higher speeds than was currently practical or even permissible with the current generation of trains running over British Railways' tracks with their comparatively tight curves and imperfect vertical as well as lateral alignments.

The key to this capability was seen as the incorporation of a high-quality tilting system that would operate entirely automatically to keep the train dynamically stable and the passengers comfortable as the whole assembly travelled round tight curves. This concept was not unique, and was under active consideration or development at much the same time by railroads in countries such as Canada, Italy and Japan. However, it was only the Canadian LRC train that was conceived in terms as ambitious as those of the ATP as in the other schemes the body was designed to tilt passively in response to the forces imposed on it rather than actively to match the tilt to the curve as the train entered it. In the APT the body-tilting system was therefore planned as a positive element of the train's control system, each of the coaches modifying its angle of tilt in relation to the camber of the track and the forces imposed on the train on the basis of sensors reporting the movement of the coach in front of it. The maximum tilt angle was 9°, and at this angle the outer side of the coach was 1ft 4in (0.406m) higher than the inner side. The premise on which the

TGV, the ETR 401 was designed for use on existing track and was therefore designed with the very small axle load of 23,148lb (10500kg), and this ensures that the operation of the train has minimal adverse effect on the track.

The most interesting feature of the train at the technical level is, of course, the tilting system designed to maximize safety and the comfort of the 170 passengers as the train rounds curves at speeds higher than those for which the track was originally created. The maximum tilt angle is 9°, and the tilt is produced actively, under the control of a system of accelerometers and gyroscopes, rather than merely passively in response to the curve and the g forces exerted on the train as it passes round the curve. The propulsion arrangement of the ETR 401 is of the

electric type, and draws current from overhead lines by means of a pantograph current collector installed on a frame mounted on one of the bogie bolsters so that it is not affected in its task by the tilting.

There have been a few accidents with the ETR 401, but in general the operation of this type of train has been moderately successful. The train first entered service on the 185-mile (298-km) route between Rome and Ancona across the Appennine mountains. The nature of this route allows the ETR 401 to develop its maximum speed of 156mph (250km/h) for only a relatively short time, but provides ample scope for the tilting system to reveal its advantages on the short-radius curves typical of any railroad system operating across a mountain range. The ETR 401's high speed offered

whole system was based in financial terms was that on journeys of more than 200 miles (322km), the APT would be able to operate at much the same speed as the French TGV but without the enormously expensive process of creating a wholly new track system. It was conservatively estimated that the development and production of the APT-P to run on existing tracks would be only about one-fifth of the cost of the TGV and its special track system.

ABOVE: British Rail's 155mph (250km/h) experimental APT (Advanced Passenger Train) began secret trials on a 4-mile (6-km) length of disused track near Derby in 1973, carrying a British Rail research team. The trial provided data for the building of two prototypes, the start of a fleet that was to cover inter-city routes.

ABOVE and LEFT: *The APT-P (P for Prototype) offered British Rail considerable capabilities, but was beset by technical problems that led to the type's cancellation. Before this happened, however, the prototype APT-P trains had revealed that their overall level of performance was genuinely excellent.*

At the conceptual level, therefore, the APT appeared to be a winner, and this fact seemed to be emphasized in that the tilting body system was only part of the complete package, whose other element was a radically improved suspension system incorporating a self-steering feature in the bogies.

British Railways requested the necessary financial package from the British government in December 1967, and in 1973 permission was given for the

OPPOSITE: British Rail's APT on a run between Carlisle and Carnforth at about 130mph (209km/h).

RIGHT: Though it suffered from a few technical difficulties, the APT-P was perhaps cancelled too promptly, for the type could have provided British Rail with an excellent high-speed passenger capability for its longer-distance services within the U.K.

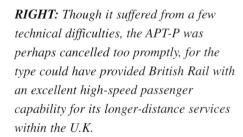

construction of the first experimental four-car set with gas turbine propulsion. This was secretly tested by British Railways, which revealed the experimental rig in 1975. This prototype was the APT-E (Advanced Passenger Train – Experimental) that successfully operated at a maximum speed of 151mph (243km/h) on the section of the main-line track west of London between Reading and Swindon and, perhaps more importantly, averaged slightly more than 100mph (161km/h) between London and Leicester.

The success of these early trials led to the granting of permission for the manufacture of three 14-car production prototype trains, each comprising two central and non-tilting power cars in which 8,000hp (5965kW) would be generated, and 12 tilting cars for use as six-car forward and rear sections each incorporating a buffet car as well as carrying 72 first- and 195 second-class passengers. Although gas turbine propulsion had originally been planned, this was now considered too expensive in terms of its fuel consumption

and, in the absence of diesel engines offering adequate power at the modest power/weight ratio that was clearly required for maximum speed and the highest possible acceleration, the decision went to electrical power. This decision was reinforced by the fact that the main routes on which the new train was designed to operate, most notably those linking London with Glasgow and Liverpool were already electrified.

The other side of the coin from a rapid acceleration and a high maximum speed is

the ability to halt quickly and securely, and for this reason the APT was planned with a hydro-kinetic braking system and disc brakes to provide deceleration to a halt from a speed of 155mph (250km/h) in a standard distance of 2,500 yards (2285m) and a maximum-effort distance of only 2,000 yards (1830m).

The first of the 14-car APT-P (Advanced Passenger Train – Prototype) trains was delivered in 1978. The performance of the train was highly impressive, but before the type could enter

ABOVE: Pre-production model of the electric-powered Advanced Passenger Train (APT), 1980.

ABOVE RIGHT: Technical trials of the APT-E (Advanced Passenger Train – Experimental) near the M1 motorway, north of London, in 1974.

service there was a catalogue of small problems to be overcome, and the type completed only one return service between London and Glasgow before the appearance of other problems, combined with the threat of industrial action, persuaded British Railways to take the type out of service and the government to postpone and finally to cancel the planned APT-S (Advanced Passenger Train – Series) full-production version. The data for the APT-P high-speed electric passenger train with advanced tilting capability included propulsion by 25,000-volt alternating current delivered via overhead catenary, step-down transformer and thyristor-based control system to four body-mounted 1,000-hp (746-kW) motors in two power cars and driving wheels by means of shafts and gearing, total weight of 1,014,942lb (460378kg), overall length of 963ft 6in (293.67m) and maximum speed of 150mph (241km/h).

Many railroads have operated within the context of automatic signalling systems since the early part of the 20th century. With many rapid transport systems now based on computer-aided operations, automatic route setting has been combined with other functions to produce operating systems that are fully automatic. Though such systems can be very advanced, most trains still need a human operator to ensure that the train is ready to depart and to give the starting signal. The world's first totally unmanned train was the VAL (Véhicule Automatique Léger), a 'light rail' rapid transit system which was opened in April 1983 in the French city of Lille. The VAL is a fully automatic system of which parts are elevated, on the surface and under the ground. Moreover, the stations on this system, pointing at least one possible way to the future, are also unstaffed. For reasons of passenger safety, the platforms have glass panelling along the edge, and this

incorporates automatic sliding doors which open in concert with the doors of the VAL train only when the latter has come to a complete halt. The rubber-tyred two-car trains are driven automatically on concrete runways located 5ft 3in (1.6m) apart. There are times, however, when the cars have to be manually driven, and for such an eventuality there is a small control panel at each end, allowing staff the ability to manoeuvre the vehicles in areas such as maintenance depots.

In Canada, a fully automated Skytrain was built to provide a link between Vancouver's two 'Expo 86' sites. Opened in

ABOVE: *Pre-production model of the APT-P electric-powered Advanced Passenger Train during a commissioning run at Beattock, Scotland, 1980.*

LEFT: *Advanced Passenger Train – Experimental (APT-E) demonstrating its body-tilting during the first series of track trials in 1973.*

ABOVE: *The passenger cars of the APT-P train ushered in a new generation of accommodation for British Railways passengers, the interior of each car being ergonomically designed for the carriage of the maximum number of passengers with adequate legroom, comparatively wide aisles, and features such as adequate tables and fold-down trays on the backs of seats. The accommodation was also, of course, heated and air-conditioned, and access and egress were achieved by doors at the ends of each car.*

RIGHT: *This prototype of the ATP, seemed to offer British Rail the opportunity, then lost, to take the lead in the provision of advanced passenger transport capability.*

ABOVE: The APT-P would have provided British Rail's market-leading InterCity longer-distance rail services with an attractive and cost-effective inducement for passengers to travel by rail rather than car or aircraft.

December 1985, the Skytrain was thus called because much of the original 6.5-mile (10.4-km) route was carried on viaducts. Like those of the VAL system in Lille, the Skytrains are designed for unmanned operation, although a number of personnel have a roving brief on the system to discourage vandalism and offer assistance to members of the travelling public. The cars, made of aluminium alloy, each turn the scales at some 31,360lb (14225kg) and have provision for 108 passengers of whom 40 are seated. Evidence of the safety consciousness of this 'light rail' system's operator is provided by the fact that the first service of the morning is operated in the standard automatic fashion but also carried a member of the staff at the front of the forward car to watch for any obstruction that may have blocked the line during the night.

Like the French and Canadian systems,

59

the Docklands Light Railway opened in London during 1987, is fully automatic. However, unlike the other two systems, the trains of the Docklands Light Railway each carry a 'train captain' with the task of checking tickets and assisting the travelling public. The train captain also gives the starting signal to the control computer and, in an emergency, drives the train from a set of controls at the front of the vehicle.

In the current age, in which the computer is becoming increasingly paramount for control functions that would previously have offered employment to people, the more advanced railroads of the world are being steadily revolutionized by the installation in their vehicles of microprocessors to detect faults and failures, and thus to reduce the possibility of accidents resulting from these defects and going undetected and therefore unreported. Locomotives are equipped with onboard computers allowing operational and status data to be read directly or transferred to the maintenance depot for action.

ABOVE LEFT: *The driver's position of the APT-P, revealing a clean and uncluttered look designed to maximize driver concentration.*

ABOVE: *A trial run of British Rail's APT-P on the West Coast Main Line. This line will probably see the first regular tilting train service in Britain, but not with the APT, with their introduction to Virgin Rail in the new millennium.*

OPPOSITE: *A British Rail InterCity 125 at Teignmouth in the late 1970s.*

INDEX

**Picture
Acknowledgements**
*Amtrak, Washington,
D.C.: pages 25, 26
*Atchison, Topeka &
Santa Fe Railroad: pages
11 below, 13 left, 14
above far right, 15 above
left
*Bombardier Inc.: page
33
*British Rail (BR): title
pages, 27 both, 29 all, 30,
31 both, 32 below, 39
below, 52, 53 right, 55, 56
both, 57 both, 58 both, 59,
60 both, 61
*Canadian National
Railway: pages 12 above
left, 13 right
*Canadian Pacific
Railway: page 12 above
right and below
*Deutsche Bundesbahn:
pages 10 below, 11 above
right, 32 above left and
right
Fiat Ferroviaria: pages 50,
51
*Finnish State Railways,
Helsinki: pages 10 above,
11 above left
*Italian State Railways:
page 47 both
*J. Dunn: page 20
Japanese National Tourist
Office: pages 22 below, 23
Military Archive &
Research Services,
Leicester, England: pages
19 right, 21, 24 both
*Netherlands State
Railway: page 14 above far
left
©Railfotos, Millbrook
House Limited, Oldbury,
W. Midlands, England:
pages 8, 9, 14 below, 15
right above and below, 17
right, 18, 19 left (P. J.
Howard), 21 above
(E. Talbot), 28 (P. J.
Robinson), 52–53 (P. J.
Robinson), 54

*Société Nationale des
Chemins de Fer (SNCF)
Paris: pages 4–5, 6, 7, 14
above centre right, 16, 17
left, 36, 37, 38, 39 above
left and right, 40 both, 41
both, 42, 43 all, 44, 45 all,
46
*Southern Pacific
Transportation Co.: page
14 above centre left
VIA Rail, Canada: pages
34, 35 both

* Prints/transparencies
through Military Archive
& Research Services,
Leicester, England

Appomattox Regional Library Systems
Hopewell, Virginia 23860
01/04

ROH